I EXPERI

I Experienced a Miracle!

A personal account of a sevenfold divine healing miracle in the city of Birmingham England 1988

of

Mrs Jean Neil

*Written by George Sensecall
a witness of her long sufferings and healing*

with Foreword by

Reinhard Bonnke

Founder-leader Christ for all Nations.

New Wine Press

New Wine Press
PO Box 17
Chichester PO20 6RY
England

ISBN 0 947852 50 6

Typeset by CRB Typesetting Services, Ely, Cambs.
Printed by Anchor Press Ltd, Tiptree, Essex.

Contents

Comment

In this book George Sensecall has recorded in some detail the life story of Mrs Jean Neil of Rugby.

Jean has been a member of the Assembly Of God Church in Rugby for over twenty years, therefore as Pastor during that period I am in a position to verify the facts related.

In reading the first sketchy outline of this book, it seemed to me a very typical story, sadly like thousands of other people and a recipe for disaster, apart from three extraordinary events!

The Bible speaks of Jesus as the key to life and at an early age Jean found that key, by accepting the Lord Jesus Christ as her own personal Saviour.

Secondly having been baptized in water by

immersion she was filled with the Holy Spirit as in Acts 2:4. Thirdly on the 12th March 1988 in the National Exhibition Centre in Birmingham, God miraculously healed her body and delivered her from a life of pain and bondage to her wheelchair.

This great miracle, witnessed by twelve thousand people, so impressed the narrator and quickened his faith in the Lord, that he was moved to write this book in the hope that it will do the same for other people in need of salvation and healing.

In recommending this book to all who are seeking deliverance from sin and sickness, I earnestly pray that God will bless it and meet the spiritual and physical need of all who read it.

Romans 10:13: '*Whosoever shall call upon the name of the Lord shall be saved.*'

V. Cunningham.
Pastor

Foreword

by Reinhard Bonnke

Twelve thousand people witnessed before their very eyes the marvellous event described in this book. Some had known her for years and seen Jean Neil's great sufferings. Nobody present when she stepped out of pain could ever surely doubt again. The day of miracles is still with us.

Jean Neil had seven afflictions. She was restored to perfect health in a few seconds of time. This was outstanding among healings, because her sufferings were outstanding. The circumstances of her cure, in the vast NEC, made it all the more spectacular and notable.

This certainly deserves a special place in the records, just as certain healings were selected for special mention among all the miracles Christ wrought. Indeed this was a real Bible-type miracle.

For this reason I am happy to endorse this book with a foreword that God shall be glorified.

Nevertheless maybe there could be one misunderstanding. It might be thought that this marvellous healing is being reported in this way because healings are so surprising and rare. In fact it is far from being so. We should never be surprised at Jesus keeping His word. There is nothing surprising either about the Almighty Christ being able to raise a crippled woman from years of pain. But the circumstances of her healing are such that many other sufferers could be encouraged to trust God. They also happened to be particularly dramatic.

Healings are not unusual today. Across the whole world God's mercies are falling and countless millions rejoice in the healing Christ, the same yesterday, today and forever. In my own world-wide 'Christ for all Nations' crusades we constantly witness the manifestation of the Spirit of God. He is restoring the sick and afflicted; cripples walk, the blind see and the deaf hear.

The moment of the healing of Mrs Jean Neil was caught with video cameras, and again God's hand was in this. He wants the whole world to see the glory of the Lord and His power, mercy and goodness. Not only is Jean's personal experience recorded in this book for all to read, but what onlookers saw has also been captured to be seen again just as it took place, for all who care to view this video now being sold far and wide.

It is time for the nations to wake up to Christ. He is striding the continents and reaching out His nail-scarred hands wherever He is preached in fullness, just as he walked in the Holy Land long ago. Jesus is alive indeed. Through the means of printing, film and video the people everywhere take heart – God has not forgotten them. He is visiting the world today – let it be known by every means.

God will bless this book, and even while people read its pages, the Holy Spirit is present to do for them what was done for Jean. It is my prayer that this shall be.

Reinhard Bonnke
January 1989

Introduction

This is a true story of the miracle of complete recovery of our friend Mrs Jean Neil, and is an account of her life of pain and anguish and tremendously deep Christian Faith even when to move was an effort. Her faith was so deep and trusting that even going to her regular Pentecostal Meeting, collapsing on several occasions, her spirit never wilted.

She was so justly rewarded by the Lord's miracle, that it has given her a new lease of life, going to the local hospital and helping to give hope to sick and crippled people in the very ward where until quite recently she had lain immovable for some weeks at a time.

I hope on reading this little book you and others may feel that trusting in the Lord brings great reward, and especially as I am an Anglican, bind all denominations close together and realise that the Lord is present in every life, regardless of denomination.

My wife, also Jean, is of the Pentecostal Tradition but that matters not as we both praise and know the greatness of the Lord and his wonderous works.

My grateful thanks to Jean for her help and to my wife for reading and criticizing, where necessary, my statements.

After some deliberation I persuaded Jean to record on tape a history of her life generally, from the time she was in an orphanage, then in service at an early age, through many traumatic experiences, to the final relief from pain and anguish lasting many years.

Her ups and downs were so numerous and I am so grateful for help and frankness.

I am deeply grateful to Mrs Margaret McStay who carefully 'sorted out' and typed the tape and corrected the errors I made as she did with my dictation at work for many years.

It is my sincere hope that all sufferers of any infirmity will find hope and faith to ease their own pain and suffering, as miracles can happen, anywhere, any time and all the time.

I have learnt having taped all Jean's statements which has enabled this book to be written, and causing me to re-run the tapes on
innumerable occasions, that Jean's sufferings
were so intense, the re-living of her life brought
tears to her eyes so often, that the miracle was
more wonderful than I ever thought possible.

Chapter 1

First Meeting

After many years as church organist at various Anglican, Methodist and Baptist Churches, my wife suggested that we paid a visit to the Lawford Road Assembly of God meeting.

I was somewhat nervous, and with the free expression of the members I felt initially that this was not my scene. I was too conservative and felt more at home in my own quiet service.

When I saw the members of the congregation praying *ad lib* and seemingly quite free and confident, I could see the devotion and sincerity of these people.

Jean sat at the front and occasionally painfully drew herself up looking more ashen with every movement.

I said to my wife, I suppose without

thinking, and of course not knowing Jean's faith and trust in the Lord, 'Who's that idiot obviously in dreadful pain? She should have more sense than to try to stand up!'

I was sternly reminded where I was.

Regrettably I could not see the Lord obviously wanted Jean to put her faith in him and to put her trust in his power to help her.

Eventually Jean had to remain seated and began to look really ill, and at times in a state of collapse.

At the end of the service Pastor Valentine Cunningham greeted my wife and I and all the members came up to us and introduced themselves. Mr Cunningham invited us to the Tuesday coffee morning which my wife accepted and I declined.

On Tuesday I drove my wife duly at 10.00 a.m. to the coffee morning and then dutifully collected her at 11.00 a.m.

I was asked to play a hymn to end the service, and thought, 'Great', now I can have a go on the Hammond Organ.

Well at last I thought maybe I should speak to Jean who was in great pain, but made very little of her great difficulty in moving. I made, as I see now a very tactless remark – 'you must

18

be mad trying to come to meetings in that condition', and all I had was a smile!

I could sense my wife was very hurt, and too late I realised how tactless I had been.

However, there was a prayer meeting at 7.30 p.m. that night, and again I was the dutiful chauffeur, collecting my wife at 9.00 p.m.

On arrival I crept in the front door and listened to ascertain if the meeting had finished!

It had not – so I stood in the area before the inner door and to a stranger's ears, strange sounds came forth. I could not understand a word!

When the meeting ended I entered the hall and met again all the members who treated me as if they had known me for years.

The Pastor told me that Roy the organist was away the following Saturday and Sunday and asked me to play for the meeting on Sunday.

I did attend and thoroughly enjoyed the meeting but was still puzzled but the utterances from members of the meeting.

On our journey home my wife explained to me, when I brought up the speaking of the members which I could not understand, and for the first time I knew that people can talk in tongues, especially when they feel the Holy

Spirit is there. Also I learned that some people have the gift of interpreting these spoken words in tongues.

The next Sunday my wife joined me for worship at our village church when the Rector confirmed my wife's thought that he was a born again Christian, which in ignorance was again explained to me!

It was a revelation to me but I still enjoyed my own service, sincerely believing that the Lord is present at any meeting, Church or where two or three are gathered together.

However we had an arrangement that I went to the Church and Assembly of God alternately.

The next time I met Jean I finally found out about her illness, and she also explained her faith and trust in the Lord and her belief that this deep trust would help to ease her suffering. She was in a state of great pain and discomfort but made little of it.

I apologised for my earlier comments, but added that I felt sincerely that she should not embark on any undue strain as many years ago I fell down a flight of stairs at my works office, and slept on 2 planks for several weeks, but luckily recovered.

We invited Jean to our house, and agreed to make a definite date for a future Tuesday.

Chapter 2

Details Begin to Emerge

Well the day arrived! My wife, Jean, was ready to go to her Pentecostal Church so we set forth to go to the Assembly of God in Lawford Road, in my two door Ford Escort, taking great care to remove the dog's blanket from the back seat.

I duly did my taxi-run and returned to collect the two Jeans at 11.00 a.m. and of course to earn my cup of coffee and biscuits after playing two hymns.

Mrs Jean Neil was getting ready to enter the car, with another lady Jessie severely crippled.

I thought it best to take Jessie home first, as I could not get two ladies in the front seat, and neither could travel in the back.

Jean was waiting with her sticks, and after

my wife got in the back seat, the struggle began!

I tried to help Jean but my efforts caused her great distress.

The journey home was satisfactory, but to get Jean out was a real feat of manouverability, but we made it.

Only after half an hour or so could I begin to realise the condition she was in. She could neither sit nor stand in comfort but she was cheerful and joking and we had a good sing-song of choruses. I cannot sing a note but the two Jeans sang quite professionally to my accompaniment.

It was very difficult to find out any real details at this stage as Jean made little of her disability.

The problem then arose that I had dreaded! The bathroom was of course upstairs, but thank God, Jean assured us that she could cope with her two sticks.

My wife and I made Jean comfortable with cushions for her to relax a while.

It was obvious that the pain was continually intense but Jean insisted she was comforted by the Lord.

I am sure that even our 13 year old dog in

her way understood, as she did not show her usual boisterous self, and just licked Jean as if to say 'I understand how you must feel'.

It was on this day that my wife and I discovered that Jean ran the Sunday School — every Sunday from 12 to 1.00 p.m., as a sideline, despite her suffering.

After a most enjoyable time the two 'Pentecostals' needed transport to the 7.30 p.m. evening meeting. I thought another disastrous 'taxi' trip, but no problems on the return journey.

Thankfully Pastor Cunningham took Jean home.

On this occasion I met a very dear lady who became a great friend of my wife and I. Mrs Green had suffered for many years and had had a very tragic life.

She is one of the nicest and kindest ladies we have ever met and despite her incapacity she is always cheerful. Her faith is so great, yet she can do so little for herself.

But I suppose this lady would need a story on its own.

Jean was so kind to her and visited her as often as she could make her way on her own rare better days.

My own faith was beginning to improve. There seemed to be so many people in this very small meeting who had such strong faith. It seemed to ease their pain and burdens. How I envied them.

Chapter 3

Jean Speaks

'I was born in the Channel Islands, Jersey, in July 1935. I was one of a large family of 13, six boys and seven girls. During the last baby's birth my mother had a massive stroke.

For a long time we children had to look after one another.

My father used to come home regularly very drunk and was most violent towards us all.

On one occasion two of my older brothers were quietly at home by the fire, when my father arrived home, drunk as usual, and started his cruel ways again. He hit them with a poker.

After this and other incidents we were all split up and sent to child centres, the girls to one and the boys to another, a long way away.

This caused us to be a separated family as my mother had to return to hospital, and it was adjudged by the powers that be that we had no senior person to care for us, least of all our father, due to his record of drink and violence.

I stayed in the nursery section of the home until I was 6 years old and was then moved back to another home with some of my older sisters.

After some years we sisters began to part, as all had the idea of living different lives.

We became strangers to each other but I did become close to my younger sister Roselle who is living near me to this day.

At the age of 15 I went into service for 12 months, then decided that I really wanted to take a Nursery Training Course, and actually took a job in the Nursery section of that same Children's Home.

This gave me great pleasure as I knew instantly how these young children must be feeling, in fact as orphans.

I successfully passed my Nursery Grading Exams and then progressed into General Nursery.

Unfortunately illness suddenly caused me to resign.

I was asked out of the blue one evening to go to a Brethren Meeting in Jersey – and along with nine other teenagers we decided to give it a try and see if we could disrupt the meeting for a lark. Unfortunately when we arrived there were only ten seats left, and right in the front row – of course we thought 'that lot had arranged it so that we would have to behave ourselves'.

The Speaker was a Brother Hockin from Cardiff and God had different ideas for me. That very night He spoke to me, and this was the very first time I realised that as this was Good Friday, Jesus had died for me. All this happened so suddenly, despite our being made to attend Church every Sunday whilst in the Childrens Home. This was the first time I had heard the Gospel and felt so strongly that it convicted me to give my life to the Lord.

It was a very strange situation because the Brethren women had to keep silent in the Church.

The only time a woman spoke in this Church was at a Woman's Own meeting or teaching in the Children's Bible class.

I met my husband through a Church magazine, St. Matthews, which had been sent from the Midlands to one of the nurses and in the end section were lists of pen friends so that if any readers were interested a letter would be appreciated from likeminded Christians.

We all thought, well why not, so we decided to pin a name with our eyes closed and John Neil was the man to whom I have been married for 30 years! After a courtship of trips to and from Rugby we named the wedding day in Jersey. We now have 4 children.

John's work caused me to move to Rugby.

Throughout my life I have had fourteen operations. Three were in Jersey for lame toes and appendicitis at the age of twenty one. Hospital life started too soon, I thought.

John and I had made arrangements to buy our own house in Rugby and it was a neat little house in Newland Street.

Before leaving Jersey I was given a letter of introduction to a Brethren Church in Rugby, but we couldn't trace it.

Fortunately I had an unexpected invitation to the Assembly of God Church in Lawford Road.

Life wasn't easy when we were first married. As the saying goes 'you do not know anyone until you live with them'.

I was led to run the first children's play scheme and also we gave the children a chance of enjoyment throughout the holidays. For over twelve years I was able to give the children, I hope, that little extra in life and things I was denied in my childhood.

But to revert to my first taste of the Assembly of God, I went frankly out of curiosity – I had been to my husband's church occasionally, but I felt there was something missing.

My immediate reaction was the friendliness of all the people at Lawford Road and their obvious love and kindness to me, as if I had known them all for years.

A lady named Mrs Tewe invited me, and an immediate friendship was formed as we were one street apart. It was a most strange meeting, as I had never been anywhere which allowed women to get up and pray without being asked. There was clapping, rejoicing etc. all strange to me.

Despite all this I went home and said to John 'I'm not going again, they are all a strange lot as they talk in Double Dutch and I can't understand what they say', but of course I now know they were speaking in tongues, being filled by the Holy Spirit.

I also felt all the clapping was somewhat irreverent, and that there seemed to be too many Alleluiahs.

The Bible says that when filled with the Holy Spirit these gifts are given abundantly. I did settle down easily and was asked if I wished to be baptised in water, which is an indication and an outward testimony that you accept new life in Christ and your old life is buried, as you rise to a new life.

I felt that I also wanted a full time job.

One day my sister in law said, 'I have some carpets for you', and if I would bring John along her husband would help us all load them up. During the carrying of the carpets, due to a foolish prank I fell on the kerb and broke the lower section of my spine.

This was the start of 25 years of great agony.

Chapter 4

The Beginning of a Life of Surgery

I was taken to the Hospital of St Cross in Rugby, where I spent 8 weeks on solid boards, hoping that the fracture would mend, but no success. The news was broken to me that an operation on my spine was urgently needed.

I had now lost the use of both arms and in addition had an operation on each arm at the same time as the spine re-setting.

The arm problems needed nerve surgery.

There the Assembly visitations, despite my short membership, and the love shown to me by the members, hit me so hard.

Never had I received such kindness and spiritual help.

Also it came back to me how these people

gave me the comfort which I had lost since the age of six.

Pastor Val Cunningham and his wife soon took the place of my parents both worldly and spiritually.

There were so many times that I would have gone astray although I did not like some of the things they said to me, but on looking back, how right they really were. I am now convinced that their guidance was from God.

At one point my marriage was very near to breaking point, but through spiritual guidance we are still happily married after 30 years, and I thank God for this. If I had not been a Christian where would I be now? Maybe in a mental home.

I had often contemplated ending my life.

It was becoming clear to me in my hospital bed that something was still very wrong with my back, despite the marvellous care I had at St Cross, and my worst fears were realised when I was informed that my whole body was to be in a plaster cast.

This was to be on for at least six months and I soon realised that I could neither sit nor stand but merely lie flat, i.e. bed-ridden.

When I was allowed home a few days after

the plaster cast was set on, it soon occurred to me how many personal problems one can encounter.

The doctors took very kindly to my 'personal' problems and even made a written comment on my records!

I had a twice daily nurse to bathe me where they could but I am sure they never discovered my feet. My feet and ankles accordingly were never washed.

However, one day the Pastor's wife noted the sore state of my feet and had no hesitation in bathing and applying some soothing cream to them daily.

This generally showed me the love she had for a new church Member. Feet aren't the prettiest things to see at the best of times, I thought.

After this long time of discomfort I was told that a further operation on my spine was needed.

I entered a second hospital, Walsgrave in Coventry.

The surgeon, Mr Whatmore, gave me a 50/50 chance but could give no positive assurance that I would again ever walk unaided.

I had complete faith and trust in the surgeon

and felt that with God on my side as well he would not let me end up paralysed.

After the operation I was very weak and many weeks passed before I could walk at all.

My feet were again treated by Mrs Cunningham and immediately it came to my mind, how humble our Lord was to wash the disciples' feet.

I did make progress, albeit not a full recovery from this operation and was offered a post as an elderly people's warden.

Chapter 5

Disaster

My new job was being warden to a block of Flats in Sun Street, Rugby on a part-time basis, which involved visiting elderly people on a daily basis in self-contained units, and requiring warden attendance on emergency call.

I soon found even on a part-time basis that visiting thirty people daily and in total climb a hundred stairs daily, was a little more that I had envisaged, to say the least.

As the days went by I began to love every minute of my work.

The people varied in temperament, sometimes from day to day.

The job to me was both exciting and interesting. No day seemed the same, something different happened all the time.

I felt that elderly people are so often left alone, but I found increasing joy in trying to make their life worthwhile and rewarding.

To my great happiness I managed to lead many of them to the Lord, and was with them when their last hour arrived.

After two years I was offered the chance of becoming a full time Warden, and each self-contained flat was to have a new intercom unit fitted, which would enable each occupant to speak to me first – instead of just buzzing the alarm light, and causing me on the odd occasion to go up thirty stairs to be told 'sorry dear, I pressed the button in error'.

Some of the calls were for genuine upsets at night, when a cup of tea and a friendly word worked wonders.

I am sure that my deep Christian faith gave me that extra patience and sympathy to make my job so very worthwhile.

Unfortunately after a few years I began to miss out in the Church.

Although I still did the Sunday School and Young Searchers League, I confess I used to use the elderly people as an excuse to miss a Meeting or two.

I know now that this was Satan trying to get me away from the Church.

I believed that the job was taking me over. The work of the Warden seemed to be so demanding, doctors needed, the sadness of patients to be comforted, Home Help problems, etc. etc.

Very often doctors and Welfare Visitors did not suffice. Residents wanted to talk to the Warden 'for only a few minutes dear,' which often turned to hours of comfort.

Sometimes the alarm bell would go in the early hours, the caller would say 'I can't sleep', and on rare occasions I would say 'neither can I nor my family, that makes six of us'. The Warden's life could be all hours, with calls in the middle of cooking the meal for my husband and four children – but I guess I had patience, even though not all the time.

During my summer holiday I devoted the time to organising local playgroups.

One of the highlights was trips to the Sea for the first time for many poorer children.

Sometimes in the summer months these play schemes lasted from 9.00 am to 4.00 pm.

Weary at night I was somehow refreshed by next morning to go through another 7 hours.

On the end of their six weeks holiday, and as I was still being on sick leave, the children asked me to continue a few more days, but I then discovered this would be without any aid from the Local Authority and I really felt I wanted more time with my family.

In addition my eldest daughter Judith had just completed her Nursing training at Northampton General Hospital and she wished me to go to the Hospital with the car to collect all her study and personal things from her place of residence, the Nurses' home.

So I decided to utilise my last weeks sick leave to go out and about with my family.

The final trip to the Nurses Home was then arranged to collect Judith's remaining belongings.

The return journey proved to be a disaster and on driving through a village, West Haddon, we had a double tyre blow-out.

The car went out of control completely and Judith, who was driving, kept the car on the road, I believe by the grace of God.

Two nearside doors were completely torn off and we finally came to a halt after cutting a telegraph pole in half!

A section of the pole cut through the

windscreen and broke my arm and caused serious head injuries. My spine was crushed, as also were both legs. My neck was also severely damaged.

In the meantime my daughter was thrown out of the car and two of my other children, by the grace of God, had only minor bruising and shock.

I felt sure God had His caring hands on us all, because the first person to arrive at the scene was the Chief Medical Officer from the hospital and in the next car was a Doctor Hynan, followed by another car containing a Senior Doctor, followed by the last car containing the Ward Sister in charge of my daughter, and three nurses. All these wonderful people were going on duty.

The arrival of such an array of medical experts certainly saved my life, as later I was told 'if you had not been moved expertly then the result could have been fatal'.

I thank God for this as I grew more confident that He was by my side.

I was taken to the Hospital of St Cross, Rugby, being the nearest.

After extensive x-rays I was advised of the total damage.

I forced myself not to sleep, as all people seem afraid to die, but my Christian faith told me if that happened I knew where I should go. I had given my life to the Lord.

The thing that hurt me most was the fear that my children might not be coming to the place I knew the Lord would take me.

They had made a commitment previously but had not gone on with the Lord.

All these things went through my mind for several days, not helped by the condition of my head injuries, also those young children who for 5 weeks had given me happiness in the play scheme.

Then the children from the Sunday School started to call to see me. The poorer ones took a sweet out of their mouth and said, 'have this, Miss, it will make you better'.

Then a young lad came with a bunch of flowers (dandelions) as he had no money to buy others.

They talked to me and one little one said 'if you had been at the extra week's Play Scheme you wouldn't have been in the car' – quite true, I thought.

I again thanked God for His care and love, the wonderful dedication of St Cross Hospital, and the Church brothers and sisters. Even some of the elderly from the Home, who I had cared for, came to see me somehow.

Then, for the first time in my life I was put in a wheelchair, which I hated.

I had this fear of being in a wheelchair, that would cause people to think I was not a human being.

However, I was now able to be taken to the Church, but due to my head injuries many a time I could not follow the message being given. It was so bad sometimes that I felt worse on leaving the meeting than the joy I had in being able to go to Church. Time and time again I was prayed for and God gave me such comfort and the need to carry on, by now I had that great feeling that God would heal me sometime.

All the time I had been in the wheelchair I knew I had to have three operations – one to the base of my spine, two – my neck area, three – have glass removed from my head, which an x-ray had revealed.

Chapter 6

The First Partial Healing

The time had come when special meetings were to be held in our own Assembly in Lawford Road, the guest speakers were Mr and Mrs Lloyd from Rotherham. They had taken several meetings in the past in our Church.

Of course, I had to be taken to this meeting in a wheelchair and it was one of my very bad days. I was feeling very depressed and I suppose if I had been left to myself I wouldn't have gone, as I was in great pain, and having most severe headaches.

I felt so low and useless as I sat in a wheelchair, and felt so ill that I could not take in the word of God – Satan seemed to be ridiculing me the whole time – saying to me 'what are you doing here? You are like a zombie'.

Being in a wheelchair in this state I could not take in the message and I felt I would have been better at home. I was being tormented the whole of the meeting, and my speech which had been so slurred became worse. At last the call came from the speaker for any sick to go out to the front, and at that time Satan really attacked me. I could not ask anyone to take me out in the chair, because my speech had gone.

The use of my arms disappeared, I could not move my chair nor make any signs to anyone. I just sat and cried.

Eventually I tried to attract Mr and Mrs Cunningham's attention which succeeded and I was wheeled out to the front and could sense that Mrs Lloyd had gleaned how I felt and the hopeless state that I was in.

Satan did not want me to be prayed for, as he knew that God was so mighty He could perhaps do some healing for me.

Mrs Lloyd prayed that I would have the restoration of my senses, so that I could take in what was being said.

I was unable to stand at all. I had a neck collar on, a surgical spinal corset, and in order to stand for a second or so I had to use crutches.

After the first prayers I felt a great surge of relief, a feeling of peace and tranquility all over.

I felt I could talk rather slowly and more prayers were offered. It appears that Mr and Mrs Lloyd had been praying for me over a long period, once they were aware of my disability. The whole congregation appeared to be in the Spirit. Suddenly I felt God wanted to tell me that I must try and stand up. I did stand quite strongly, only holding my crutches lightly – and then a voice came to me – 'Do away with your crutches and take off your collar.' I suddenly recalled that I had earlier said to Mrs Lloyd 'I must give you my collar, and the crutches'.

I felt I must do this, but feared I might fall. 'Do not worry', said Mrs Lloyd – 'we will hold you if necessary'. So I removed my collar and my neck just seemed to sag. There was no support left, my crutches were handed over. Prayers were said for me, and I felt the power of God in my body.

I cracked to the floor under the power of the Holy Spirit and lay there for some time.

Then I came to and realised I was being helped to my feet. I could walk very slowly, yet nervously, with no collar and no sticks, first with a gentle support from Mr and Mrs Lloyd, up the aisle of the church and back again.

I had a feeling of relief and that God had begun the healing that very night.

However I still needed the wheelchair after my first partially aided steps. This first healing was on a Saturday night. On the Sunday we had another visiting speaker. Mr Phillip Bateman at the Gospel Service, and I felt I must go out for prayer again, and to my surprise and by the power of God I got out of my wheelchair and with the aid of my 2 sticks I hobbled to the front seat. Immediately Phillip Bateman saw my state he laid his hands upon me.

He prayed in the name of Jesus that I would have a complete recovery and once again I felt a tremendous heat go through my whole body, neck, spine and legs and I immediately knew that it had been God's wish that I went for prayer that day.

I remember getting up from the seat, having such new power in my legs that I actually ran as far as the church door and back, not with terrific force but I certainly ran. I was happily rejoicing because I knew God had begun my healing.

The next day I received a call to enter

hospital for an operation and I phoned to explain that I was recovering. It was suggested I still kept the appointment merely for a routine check-up.

I was seen by Mr Whatmore, the surgeon at Walsgrave Hospital, Coventry. I felt an awful fraud, as when I previously left Hospital I had a neck collar, corset, crutches and a wheelchair – and now I walked in albeit very slowly and unaided.

The nursing staff who knew my earlier condition were amazed.

X-rays were carried out and the medical team were astonished – something very strange had taken place, I knew God had performed a miracle. All that was needed was small manipulation of my spine.

I was allowed home the next day.

My nickname was 'the miracle walking woman. We don't know how she did it'. But I knew.

After a few more weeks of recuperation, needed because of my general weakness, I returned to my work as a Warden.

I was very concerned because I had been able to attend some meetings and then I had a definite call from God to give up my work as a

Warden and take up work for Him, particularly for the youngsters in the Church. This did puzzle me, as I was already working again for the Sunday School and the Youth meetings on Wednesday nights, but perhaps He thought I was not in it heart and soul.

Maybe I was not doing enough to help the Church.

The problem was I had a good job, although my husband had a disability, good wages, good residential accommodation, a telephone and car – what more could I wish for?

Why was God asking me to give up all this I asked myself? Surely I was doing my part already in the Church, after all I had been through.

I challenged God, asking Him to give me a few more years and when my family were older, perhaps I could give my all then.

God had a different purpose in my life and I learned a lesson I shall never forget.

Two days later I had a serious heart attack and was rushed into hospital. The Pastor came to the hospital and found me wired up to all sorts of strange apparatus.

I told the Pastor all of God's message and that I felt the heart attack had been necessary.

'Jean', he said, 'I have had a feeling for a long time that your job was "taking over" and you were losing out spiritually.'

I said 'Lord, if I come through this I will give up work and give my services wholly to your wishes'. I hesitated again and had two more attacks in hospital, which left me with angina. I knew I had to work for the Lord.

My notice was handed in and reluctantly accepted by the Local Authority.

Chapter 7

From Warden Accommodation to Newbold

After leaving Sun Street Sheltered Accommodation, I was rehoused by the Local Authority on Newbold Estate, Rugby.

We lived here for a year but my health deteriorated considerably. The house and area was so damp and because of angina and bronchitis I had to have treatment seven times in the year and my breathing became more and more difficult.

Newbold was a most pleasant area, with very nice people, but, I felt too long a distance from my Church. The bus route was not very helpful and I felt it was unfair to expect the pastor to collect and return me twice on Sunday and on Wednesday nights.

My breathing worsened and I could not walk any great distance.

In the meantime, as I had dreaded, a third operation was to be performed on my spine to relieve tension after the second operation.

To my relief I made quite a quick recovery.

One evening as I was attending a prayer meeting I had a feeling that someone was placing a hand on my shoulder. I was in an angina attack at the time, and my breathing was in a frightening state.

I turned to one of the Church sisters behind me and said 'Did you tap me on the shoulder? Do you want something?' I asked. 'No Jean,' came the reply, 'I was just praying for you. Perhaps the Lord was touching you,' she said.

I felt the Lord had spoken to me again, this time at a very small gathering.

It proved that when two or three are gathered together the Lord can be present with His wonderful healing powers.

I was wearing a heart patch which was changed daily – it was a form of heart pacer – and in addition I now had to regularly use an inhaler as my breathing was worsening.

The next Sunday morning at the Breaking of Bread Service as I was adjusting my heart regulator a voice seemed to say I no longer needed this thing. I did not and forthwith got rid of it.

I still had to use the inhaler if a spell of bronchitis came on.

My doctor however told me I must move to another area, as if I continued in Newbold I would have to spend more time in hospital for my breathing problems.

The move came soon to a new house in Oliver Street nearer the town and only a short trip to the Assembly.

Two years ago I had more serious back trouble and this was to be the most difficult time in my life.

The pain was more severe than before, now in addition I began to have blackouts, as if for good measure.

I was then given heart tablets to be taken regularly without fail.

My eyesight was failing, to add to my misery, caused, I was told, by the side effects of so many tablets.

I could not read my Bible or hymn book, and I wondered why this had to happen to me yet again.

The great consolation I had at this stage was

the realisation that over the years I had learned so much of the word of God.

Only now did I realise the horror of my inability to read my favourite book, the Bible.

Much worse was to come – back into the Hospital of St Cross in Rugby, flat on a hard base, on traction treatment – manipulation, and regular painkilling injections. The doctors and staff were wonderful; everything seemed to be tried to ease the pain.

I spent six months in hospital and was eventually taken to Walsgrave Hospital in Coventry, where I was told there was no further treatment they could advise to be safely carried out. Operations could not be considered as there was always the risk of total paralysis.

This was a great blow to me – I could have any equipment to help, wheelchair, crutches again, painkillers galore. But what a life, I thought.

I even had a special 'high level' toilet seat! bath table equipment etc. I cannot speak too highly of the surgeons, doctors and staff at both hospitals and all the Welfare People. I began to feel a V.I.P. Such housework I did was by hobbling around hanging on to sticks and furniture.

Cooking was nearly impossible. Jobs which normally took a few minutes took an hour. I tried to do some washing to ease the burden on my family but the pain became unbearable at times.

The most difficult thing was when kind people tried to help me move around, and all I could do was scream with pain.

My screams had been heard in Church, in shops and in the street and brought odd looks from people.

Of course I was now back in the wheelchair again, waiting sometimes impatiently for someone to call to take me out.

I could not manoeuvre the chair myself because of the strength leaving my arms. The pavements and kerbs were very uneven in parts which did not help matters.

Again my doctor told me nothing more could be done. That was a great morale booster, I thought, but my doctor was kindness itself, and I felt only a miracle could help.

I am glad we have a miracle doctor, Our Lord.

Medical science has not got all the answers, but Jesus has.

I began to get so low in hope that, yes, if I

had not been a Christian I might have taken my life.

At times I felt I may have been stupid and asking for trouble in going to the meetings, as George also told me and upset me at times, until he learnt to know my faith and trust in the Lord. This altered his outlook and he along with his wife supported me in the hope of healing.

As a last resort I made a private appointment to see a Mr Stephen Eisenstein, a Consultant Surgeon at Oswestry Hospital, and after a thorough examination, test and x-rays, I was told in detail the disastrous state of my spine.

I would have to undergo major surgery to fuse bones from my hips and a large risk element would be involved.

My hip x-ray showed considerable distortion and my left leg was reduced by nearly two inches, due to the hip problem. This had caused my right leg to be bent due to the increased weight and pressure put on it.

I was hoping that this fine surgeon could give me an assurance of success – but I soon realised that this was not safely possible.

With my record of heart, bronchitis and angina, I was known as a high risk patient.

If the operation could have been carried out I would have been in specialist care for at least 12 months.

I would also have had to learn to walk again – I think I did not realise fully the implications but still felt there may have been a slight hope of some success.

I would have grasped at any straws at the time, as the pains were so intense, but throughout all this God had taught me to be humble, and to feel for others, and I began to realise that I had more love for the sick than ever before – God only allows you to bear so much and he knows what to do at the right time, because the great day of my healing was to come.

At this point I must thank the Church members for their help and understanding and especially Pastor and Mrs Cunningham, who were always at hand with their loving care, and the use of their car, waiting so very patiently, with a look of despair, as I got in or out of the car, in agony. They knew they were powerless to help me, and the slightest 'error' on their part would bring instant screams from me.

Oh, how I thank God that they were there, to get me in or out of the Church, and to pray for me.

No words can ever express the appreciation in my heart for their help.

I believe my Christian faith stood me in good stead throughout my long ordeal.

God gave me strength despite my condition to still help in the Sunday School and Youth Groups. I am sure he honours us as we honour Him.

I think about five weeks passed before my actual healing.

One Saturday night I had a definite dream. I saw in detail the whole operation that could be performed at Oswestry. I heard a conversation between the surgeons and nurses that if they could not speed it up I would die! My whole family came to the hospital and were told it was too late.

I had this dream two nights later again, and told Pastor and Mrs Cunningham that I was scared that I should have the operation.

He felt that it was not right to have the operation even though his family were influential in getting an early specialist appointment.

With these misgivings arising from my dreams, there came another mercy from God, in the shape of another dream or vision. That dream I must describe in the next chapter.

Chapter 8

The Great Moment of Healing

Before I describe this vision, there is another event that must be mentioned. The evangelist Melvyn Banks was conducting a special mission at Daventry. He is well known for his ministry to the sick by the laying on of hands and has seen many mighty miracles. I had an opportunity to attend and decided to go.

For three nights my faithful pastor, and 'chauffeur' Mr Cunningham had helped me into his car and driven me there. The pain was greater than it had been and I experienced more stiffness than ever. Mr Banks prayed for me each night.

There was benefit. I began to hobble along without sticks. But I was still 'lopsided', twisted over, and had pain right up to the third meeting on the Friday. My friends Jean and George came that night and therefore witnessed my leaving my wheelchair.

With this encouragement, came my dream. I had never been in the National Exhibition Centre, Birmingham, but one night I 'saw' this place. It was to be as I saw it. It seats 12,000 people. Rows of invalid chairs had been wheeled near to the main rostrum. I saw the evangelist Reinhard Bonnke go and pray for a lady in her chair. She got up hesitantly, then sat down again. He prayed a second time and then she rose, and presently began walking, though slowly and gingerly.

Next, in my dream, my turn came. Prayers were offered and I experienced the power of God flowing through me. I got up from the wheelchair and ran and ran and ran. Vividly I saw the word 'PAIN' following me like a threatening enemy. My dream ended with tears of rejoicing all around me, and I was praising the Lord.

The Great Day arrives, 12th March 1988

A great Pentecostal Rally had been announced in the NEC for this day. My husband had been given the use of transport, actually an ambulance, to take a group of young people and members there from Rugby to Birmingham, about one hour's drive. The preacher that day was to be Reinhard Bonnke.

They got me into the hall, and I sat in my wheelchair with a whole row of chairs both sides of me. There were two meetings, afternoon and evening. Following the first one we had a teabreak.

Then we had the evening meeting – the word of God was mighty that night, addressed very strongly to the young people. Then hundreds of young people came forward and made a commitment to the Lord throwing hundreds of cigarettes and drugs on to the platform when the appeal was made.

They were being counselled at the side, and THEN –

Mr Bonnke said 'I will now pray for the sick. Who is tired of being sick?'

During this time I was praising God, because two of my church youngsters had gone forward to make a commitment in front of 12,000 people.

I said to myself, 'Oh Lord, if I am not healed tonight I still praise you because of these two youngsters.' In fact I was oblivious as to the rest of the world momentarily.

A lady from the front had a word from Mr Bonnke that she may be healed.

Just as in my vision some weeks ago, this lady got up unaided and sat down again. 'Get up and walk in the name of Jesus', Mr Bonnke said. The lady shook her head and hesitantly got out of her wheelchair than sat back in it again – more prayers were offered for her once again – and eventually the lady stood up slowly, nervously and walked to the front. At this time my eyes were closed and then I felt two hands on my shoulders a voice saying 'open your eyes' and there was Reinhard Bonnke saying, 'I believe the Lord is going to do something mighty tonight'. I did not tell him of my vision.

I suddenly became so terribly stiff, more than ever before and said to myself – 'Well, Lord, if you want me out of this chair you will have to do something MIGHTY.

The way I feel now I shan't be able to run as I saw in my vision.'

He again prayed for me, I got up from my chair and slumped to the floor and felt a tremendous peace within me. Mr Bonnke asked

'How do you feel?' I said 'just as if I am coming out of an anaesthetic after an operation'.

'Do not look at anyone else.'

'Do not think of anyone else', said Mr Bonnke.

'Now think of Jesus. Confine your thoughts to the Lord', he said.

Again he prayed, finally saying, 'In the name of Jesus start walking'.

I suppose I was just flabbergasted, to be told to walk, no sticks, nothing at all.

My husband was worried, but was assured that all would be well as the people and Mr Bonnke would be there if anything went wrong.

I was again prayed for and at that very moment I felt a burning power go through my whole body, almost as if my short leg was being stretched back to normal.

My hips shook and straightened, a hot searing pain ran down my spine. My husband was shouting aloud, 'she'll fall, she'll fall.'

Suddenly as if something had exploded behind me I ran – and ran, shouting and praising the Lord with every step, with tears streaming down my face. All I now wanted to do was find my pastor and his wife and the party from my Church. Then I had to find my husband again. People were cheering, crying and praising the Lord – it seemed like all 12,000 had joined in.

Suddenly a host of young people were looking for a 'lady in a red beret'. Well it had fallen off in the rush. I said to them, 'Here I am'.

Still minus the beret I was being sought by Mr Bonnke. 'Where's that lady gone?' he cried out. Eventually I got back to the platform with my husband who embraced me, both of us in floods of tears, 'I never want to see you like you were so crippled again'.

I told Mr Bonnke that I had had operations etc. etc. and he knew nothing of this. I was then asked to get my husband to help me bring the wheelchair on to the stage. At the back of the stage were some steps to be climbed, which I negotiated with no difficulty.

I was completely free of all pain, aches and numbness in my joints.

We reached the stage and my husband and I were still absolutely choked with emotion through the work God had done.

Still tears were streaming down our faces, yes indeed tears of joy.

Reinhard Bonnke then spoke to me, asking me how long I had been in a wheelchair. He said to my husband, 'you have been pushing your wife around in a wheelchair for 2 years, I gather. Well now she can push you around'. He embraced my husband saying, 'I do not mean that seriously, it is just good to see what the Lord has done'.

My husband said he felt very relaxed in the presence of God and Mr Bonnke, and was able to speak quite freely.

I then witnessed to all the people present how ill I had been and for so long, detailing the whole series of operations I had been through. I told them all what God had done for me. Reinhard Bonnke told the 12,000 that after he had prayed for the first lady, he was reminded by the Holy Spirit that the lady he had seen in a vision would be healed, and he recalled how I was just running over to him. That was why he was so confident I would be healed that night.

Then I stood for a few seconds shouting aloud the praises of the Lord – and then suddenly leaping around the stage – because I was so elated my strength was growing and I knew that I was free from all pain.

Reinhard Bonnke then asked me to demonstrate at the front of the stage so that by my actions the people would know I had been healed.

The whole mass of the 12,000 were standing and shouting and singing praises.

I did a repeat of my earlier dancing and jumping just to convince everyone present of God's miracle.

Tears of joy came again, the more I realised what had happened to me the more they rolled down my cheeks.

The amazing thing that occurred to me, even with the many miracles in the Bible, even the raising of the dead, was that here was I cured of so many sicknesses all at once.

Nowhere could I recall more than one miracle happening to one person at any time.

My miracle had indeed cured SEVEN ILLNESSES ALL AT ONCE.

I thought, when God starts something He does a hundred percent work, everything to the full.

All His promises are fulfilled – I recall 'I will heal you and deliver you from all illnesses'.

The rejoicings continued and I even forgot that I had brought the wheelchair with me. I had to be reminded it was at the back of the stage. I really didn't want to have anything to do with it, but thought I must return it to where it came from.

People now started to come and embrace me and I remember one young lad coming to me. He said 'I said to the Lord – Lord I have been a Christian for a long time, but I do not see a lot in it. Today however He has shown me something, in fact, so mighty as to hold me deeper in the Christian Faith.

'Without my witnessing your miracle cure, I would have gone back into the world.'

With tears streaming down his face he added, 'Jean I will never challenge the Lord again. He is mightier than ever in my eyes. I shall now work more for God than ever before'.

This one lad was an example of maybe thousands of others at the moment who had been drawn deeper in faith to the Lord.

Pastors, Leaders of Churches from all denominations have since stated they were so joyful and blessed the Lord for what they had seen.

The Lord had in fact turned the NEC 'upside down'. He had demonstrated His might works and powers when people put their trust in Him.

After a lot of photography people wanted to talk to me and I had to push my way through the crowds to reach the ambulance to take me home.

It was on reaching the ambulance that I saw again all my own people waiting for me, thinking I was lost. They were all rejoicing. Even the youngsters were amazed, and all embraced me. Then they were crying with joy, shouting aloud 'Jean, you've been healed'.

Words were inadequate, I found I just could not explain how I felt.

I wondered how my husband John felt in his own heart as he drove us home.

He had taken me to the NEC in a wheelchair in the ambulance on one of my very bad days, and then he drove me home with the wheelchair folded up and me free from all pain and incapacities.

On arrival home I recall walking into the house and running up the stairs.

My 17 year old daughter and her boyfriend just stood there open mouthed.

My daughter said, 'Mum, whatever has happened to you?' I was able to explain but I think she was unable to take it all in. She could not believe what she was seeing.

We then all rejoiced and Sharon said, 'Mum I can't really believe it', and her boyfriend obviously shocked said, 'I don't understand, you will have to explain it in more detail. I have never heard anything like this before'.

Then my son arrived home. He was astounded to see me walking normally and pain free.

The drawn look on my face had gone, ageing me – so he noticed the immediate change in expression – as the Sunday school said, 'once you were old and now you are young, Miss!'

The ageing face, short leg, out of place hip, bent back had all disappeared. I suppose I must have looked a new woman to everyone.

Now all I want to do is to praise God for what He has done for me, to tell people and give witness to Him in the street.

I know I would have been thankful just for part healing but the Lord had made me like new, all of me.

The next morning, Sunday, as I always had kept the Lord's day as one of rest and prayer, it was with great joy and a bright stride in my legs that I walked the half mile to the 9.00 am prayer meeting. I walked with great joy and was singing and praising the Lord as I made my way.

I just wanted to use my 'new' legs and walk and walk.

It was great to be able to enter the meeting on my own, no fuss, no chair, no sticks for support.

The look of surprise on the children's faces as they came to Sunday School is something I shall never forget.

Later it came to my ears that some of the young ones had invited their friends and relatives to come to see our teacher. She was old but now is young over again.

My own young grandchildren ran to the car as Sunday School ended. They called out to my daughter, 'Mummy, Mummy, you should see our Nannie. She was all old and now she's all young and can jump about and she's all little and nice now. She's all better and Jesus made her better in Birmingham, and she can now pick us up and love us.'

I felt a lump in my throat because their remarks made me think that I had never before been able to pick them up or nurse them on my knee or play with them.

When your own grandchildren make such remarks, it made me think how old I must have looked, like an elderly bent lady, so crippled was I.

Naturally I suppose it was strange after over

two years to see me upright, running and walking naturally.

From that Saturday and week after week people who had known me for years could not believe their eyes when they saw me briskly walking and running across the road, without my chair and bent body.

The Friday following my healing was my usual appointment with the doctor.

He was most perturbed at my calling on him because of my condition when he last saw me.

When I walked into the surgery the receptionist was astonished. At first she really didn't know what to say. She was a fairly new arrival but knew my case.

When my name was called to see Doctor West he was so taken back when I walked briskly in unaided and looking so well that he seemed to be almost speechless. Then he said, 'Jean, what has happened? Have you seen another Doctor or something? I know you had an appointment at the Spinal Hospital in Oswestry but they couldn't have healed you as quick as that'.

'No,' I replied, 'I have been to a doctor. His name is Doctor Jesus. He has been working for centuries and doesn't give up.'

I thank the Lord for all Doctors, Nurses, Ancilliary Staff in any capacity, because I believe God has given them a work of genius and care to look after the sick. I shall be forever indebted to these people.

Surgeons, I believe, need the expertise and skilful hands that God has given them to carry out the intricate work that has to be done.

Some Doctors and Surgeons will say that they operate, but God heals.

Even non-believers, I think, must deep down realise that surgeons do their dedicated works, but also wonder who heals the wounds or scars. It must be God.

Doctor West said to me, 'Well, Jean, I did say to you some weeks ago I wish I was a miracle doctor, but obviously you have found one. I am so very happy for you'.

He then asked me to wait in the Surgery a while so that he could fetch his partner. Doctor Sharman arrived, who had also treated me and they both agreed that a miracle must have been performed. Certainly I looked that well.

Doctor West then said, 'Well I must write to Oswestry and cancel the operation and tell them it is not necessary now due to a divine healing.'

Two weeks later I had an appointment at the opticians, and for the first time for many years I could read the bottom line.

The opticians report was that there was a remarkable improvement in my sight.

My next appointment was at the St Cross Hospital to see the surgeon and I was to be 'wheeled in' by the nurse, but I had walked to the Hospital.

The nurse could not control her laughter and I think perhaps the specialist was *not* amused.

However, Mr Williams then saw me standing behind him in full health.

He had seen me previously and had told me that there was nothing to be done that could guarantee any improvement in my condition.

Thanks to his previous care I had to wear the dreadful corset, which gave very little relief.

Without hesitation he tore up my appointment card saying, 'Jean, I do not need to see you again. I do understand your healing. I know and have heard of such things and I praise God you had such a great night of healing'. I was then fully discharged from the Hospital.

Chapter 9

What Does the Future Hold For Me?

There are many sceptical people in this world today who say, 'seeing is believing'. Let these people know what has really happened by seeing the end product.

Even when specific details are given there are still signs of disbelief in some eyes.

However, in Rugby people got to know me in the streets, at Church and through my voluntary work, despite my handicap in the wheelchair and hobbling painfully around. Now when they see me walking and rushing around normally they begin to wonder how the doctors can do such a great thing in a few days. They knew I had to have another operation, so who has done this great thing? They have no answer to this unless they believe in miracles, and those that understand know only the Lord can do this.

It gives the sceptics plenty of food for thought.

This is living proof that the Word of God is true.

I believe God has done more for me. I now am able to go to St Cross Hospital and help the nurses and other workers who once nursed me in the Hoskyn Ward.

I have been in those beds lifeless, feeling weak and in constant pain. Now I am able to comfort others in the same beds and tell them of the power of the Lord, and what He has done for me.

I know the pain they have to bear and God has given me the health to care for and help console those suffering.

I minister to and pray for these people. It seems to ease their own pain, when they know of my past life.

God, I feel sure, will open other doors for me to witness in other churches and meetings, in the streets, market and town of Rugby and further afield.

People time and time again meet me in the streets and I let them know exactly what had brought about my restoration to health.

'God has performed a miracle', I say.

Whilst playing with my grandson in Caldecote Park in Rugby recently a young couple were asking about my healing, recognising me from my picture in the local paper. My little grandson, Roy who is five years old, spoke to these people with great assurity. 'My Nana paid a doctor a lot of money to do something for her but he couldn't do anything. He didn't heal her, and you know Jesus didn't take any money, but Jesus healed her'. My three year old grandson piped up, 'Yes, I love Jesus because he healed my Nanny and He had no money. I do love Him because my Nana can play with me now, and she's all young and nice. She was old and horrible!'

My daughter, these youngsters' mother, was recently showing them the video of the healing. Other neighbours were invited to see the healing.

People on seeing the healing video are deeply touched and end up in tears.

My whole family are relieved that I am now out of pain and misery.

The three year old grandson, on seeing the healing at the end of the video, the part where I am running back to my husband and in tears, now gets up and says to the television, 'Nanny, don't cry because Jesus loves you and loves you, and you are all better now, and you can run and walk'. Then he noticed his grandad was in tears as well and said 'What's grandad crying for? That's stupid. He wasn't sick. Nana's better now. You should be happy not crying'.

When Reinhard Bonnke was praying over me for the second time and pointing out that the Lord would open more doors for me, I went down with the power of the Spirit. My husband, for whom this was a new experience wavered a little, and he felt a tremendous power surge through his body. My grandson again piped up, 'why is Nana asleep on the floor, when grandad didn't want to sleep?'

"Out of the mouths of babes and sucklings, and a little child shall lead them".

It is true that children without understanding speak the truth.

In spite of him not knowing what was happening he just marvelled and rejoiced that the Lord had healed me.

He wanted to know why Nana couldn't have a bed. Why did she have to sleep on the floor?!

The Saturday after the video was seen, when I went into the house the three year old, Ricky, informed me he had seen the video and my daughter said he had tried to control me on the T.V. screen.

I believe God has spoken to the young people as well as the old members of the Assembly.

For a long time now I have felt God has given me a working ministry amongst the children, also probably due to my early childhood in a Home, and He has made me feel that He gives me more and more faith in His mighty powers.

The word of God has become stronger in me, my confidence has grown and I am speaking and witnessing to more and more people as the weeks go by.

If after reading the book there are still sceptics and scoffers I would say to you 'BEWARE'.

The day that the story of this miracle was published in the Rugby Advertiser, my photo was displayed on the front page.

A young Catholic lad who worked in a factory, who I met later, was seen to be mocking my picture. He had made a go-kart out of my chair and put a halo over my head, and was about to write something else after noting that I was a devout Christian.

Suddenly the power of God struck him, and he just slumped into a chair and became violently ill, so ill in fact that he had to be taken home.

For two whole nights he had dreadful nightmares and could not eat. What little he did consume he brought back, violently sick.

He became so ill and unhappy that his mother in desperation found out my address and brought her son to see me on the Monday. Obviously they were a religious family and had been told their son had mocked a holy woman.

This was right, as I had become a child of God.

This lad had not only mocked me and what had been done for me, but more seriously mocked GOD.

The lad had come to ask my forgiveness. I had nothing to forgive him for, but when it is done to GOD and as well as God's children then there is a great difference.

I believe God spoke to him and his mother.

The lad said, 'if I ever see a photo of you again, I know now I will never mock Jesus again'.

My belief is that this was a warning to anyone who mocks the power of God, the healing hand of God and all God's work, because what God has done as recorded in the Bible is still being done today.

God is as mighty now as he ever was before.

I have already started my ministry in the Hospital of St Cross, Rugby, helping the sick in some way.

I thank God for the privilege of being able to do this work for him, visiting other Churches and speaking of God's power in all things.

I try to explain to people who know of God, but do not understand His power and strength and love of us all.

One of my great pleasures was to meet and work with the Rev. George Canty of Hall Green, Birmingham and I believe this is the beginning of a new ministry that God has for me.

I just pray that I never look at my healing just to my own benefit, but to the benefit of God, and again I can now work solely just for God.

When God wants us to work for Him He wants us to be in full health to do so.

Sometimes I suppose we can bring sickness on ourselves through our own stupidity. I feel I have hindered my own healing in the past and misused my body. Now I just pray that God will lead me in everything I do and I will never stop giving him the glory and honour due to His name.

I thank God that 32 years ago I did not choose Him, but He *chose me* and I believe that when I look into my life now, how God has led me day after day week after week month after month year after year He has had a purpose in my life.

I have let Him down many times, but I thank God He never leaves us or forsakes us, and I quote the text given to me from Proverbs the day I went through the waters of Baptism.

'In all thy ways acknowledge him, and he shall direct thy paths'.

I believe that even to this day He is directing the path he wants me to go.

Chapter 10

Go and Tell

Since commencing the Book Jean has been inundated with invitations for her to make personal appearances, and my phone has rung continually. (Jean is not on the phone at present.)

With Central T.V. (Focus), Nottingham Radio, a personal call from Michelle Guiness etc. etc. life has been quite hectic.

It has all been worthwhile. I am sure Jean has a healing ministry, and already she has given hope to many sufferers.

Apart from her hospital work in the wards, including Hoskyn Ward where she suffered so often and so long, her ministry of the Lord's word has brought joy and happiness to so many sufferers and their own visitors have seen the

Lord as never before, in fact some for the first time.

I believe Jean has been healed by the power of the Lord to enable her to minister and help others, and lead more and more people to Him.

I went with Jean and my wife recently to a local Christian group meeting at a place called 'The Barn Fellowship' in Barry Turner's home, in Dunchurch called Guy Fawkes House. Jean sang and spoke of her life and suffering and ultimate healing and the power of the Lord was most strongly present.

Jean prayed for many people at this meeting and I was so impressed with the atmosphere that I realised I did not know the Lord as much as I ought.

I pray that I will get daily nearer to Him and learn more and more so that I can know I am one of His children.

Jean's healing has already been described in a German magazine and I hope and pray this book will reach a very wide area, as the more people realise the power of love and devotion our Lord shows to all, then the world will be a better place. If only all people know him more.

A video tape has been produced by Christ for All Nations, and already has gone world-wide.

Many of our friends of all denominations have seen it, and have been so blessed by its great message of faith and trust in the Lord. They have gone away so excited by the truth of God's wondrous works, that their lives have been changed.

My wife and I have accompanied Jean on several occasions to various meetings, such as at the Stratford-upon-Avon Baptist Church, which was filled to capacity recently.

Jean exercised her healing ministry, and the power of God soon became evident, as many were indeed touched by the Lord.

In the afternoon Jean was taken to see a Church member in a Hospital in Leamington Spa who was seriously ill with back trouble, and on traction.

Immediately she left, he was able to get out of bed, and walked to the door, and praise God, one week later he walked into his church, to the astonishment of the congregation.

On another occasion, at a meeting in the Baptist Church at Radford Semele, Leamington Spa, again before a capacity congregation, the power of God soon became evident, and an elderly lady, confined to a wheelchair, was prayed for, and she slowly arose out of the chair, and at first walked hesitantly, gaining strength and faith, eventually walking slowly but confidently around the church. She told me she could not stop, and had no intention of returning to the chair!

In addition one hand was quite useless, and we have been told that she is now concentrating on improving the 'new' use of her hand, to the utter astonishment of the staff of the Home where she has resided for many years.

Jean has returned from a two week journey to Paris and many French towns, where her ministry was given to all denominations.

Future journeys include for three weeks to South Africa, and no doubt many other nations.

Conclusion

I have faithfully tried to write this from tapes
made by Jean over a long tiring period, which
at times has caused her considerable distress in
recounting her life.

We have overcome various problems from
time to time and I have endeavoured to tran-
scribe from such tapes as honestly and authen-
tically as possible the direct statements made
from the heart by Jean.

I hope that having read this book it will give
you hope and inspiration. Having gone through
this at times painful experience, I feel it has
done a tremendous amount of good for me, and
has brought me much nearer to the Lord in my
own thoughts and way of life.

I would like to say that whilst playing organs

in various Churches in the area Jean's story has brought very firmly back to my mind my wife Jean's favourite hymn – 'Be Still' by Dave Evans.

Be still for the presence of the Lord
The Holy one is here,
Come bow before him now with reverence and fear,
In him no sin is found
We stand on holy ground
Be still for the presence of the Lord
The Holy one is here.

Be still for the Glory of the Lord is shining all around
He burns with holy fire, with splendour is he crowned
How awesome is the sight our radiant King of light
Be still for the glory of the Lord is shining all around

Be still for the power of the Lord is moving in this place.
He comes to cleanse and heal to minister his grace
No work too hard for him
In faith receive from him
Be still for the power of the Lord
Is moving in this place.

Finally I would like to say a big thank you to our marvellous local paper the Rugby Advertiser, to the Editor and wonderful reporter Sue Lary without whose publicity initially and generous help throughout this book may never have been published.

I couldn't have undertaken the transcribing of the tape and scribbled notes without the valuable help of my dear wife Jean. Many times she has corrected me when I made errors and irrelevant comments – she sorted out masses of notes and scraps of paper all to help the completion of this book.

My wife adds these words: 'As a Christian friend of Jean I praise God for what He has done in her life. I have cried with her in her great pain and suffering, but now I rejoice with her in this mighty work of healing that God has done'.

I quote this text from the Bible: '*Be still and know that I am God*'.

So often we limit the Power of God but He is indeed a mighty saviour and He cares and loves each one of us.

This true story of my friend Jean proves that with God ALL THINGS ARE POSSIBLE.

I pray that after reading this book you will know a measure of the blessing and love of God in you own heart and life.

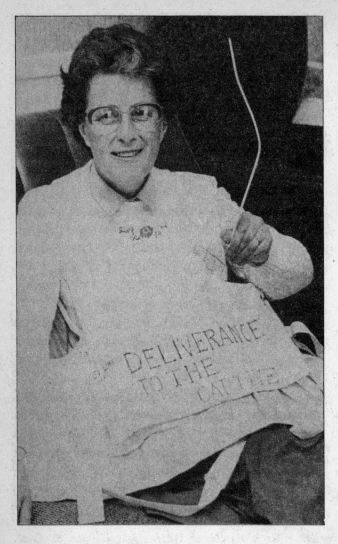

Jean holding a section of the steel shaped corset. Corset on Jean's knees!
By kind permission of the *Rugby Advertiser*.

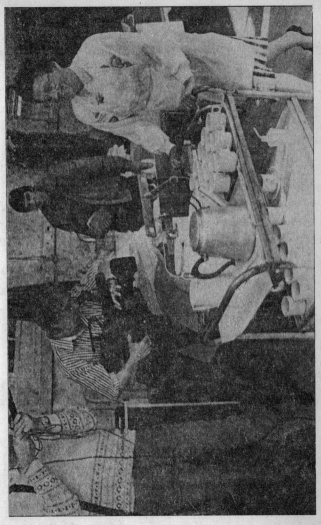

Serving tea in the Hoskyn Ward, Rugby Hospital St. Cross, where Jean was a patient several times, with T.V. technicians from Christ for All Nations.
By kind permission of the *Rugby Advertiser*.

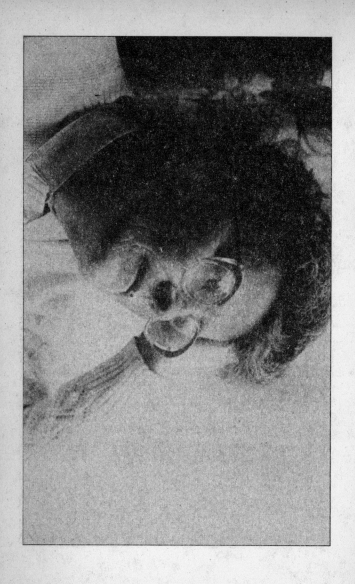

Deep in thought, for prayer.
By kind permission of the *Rugby Advertiser.*

Another jump for joy in the Lord in Jean's back garden.

KJ1972

For Further Reading

Foundations for a Healing Ministry. *Tom Marshall*. Sovereign World.

How you can heal the sick. *Stuart Gramenz*. Sovereign World.

Populating Heaven. *Reinhard Bonnke*. Sovereign World.

Alive Again. *Bill Banks*. New Wine Press.

Delivered from depression. *Liesl Alexander*. New Wine Press.

God's Gift of Healing. *Fred Smith*. New Wine Press.

Risen with healing in His Wings. *Peter Scothern*. New Wine Press.

Distributed by

Sovereign World Books/New Wine Press, PO Box 17, Chichester PO20 6RY.

Sovereign World Australia Pty Ltd, 6 Wambiri Place, Cromer, NSW 2099, Australia.

Heyes Enterprises, PO Box 24-086, Royal Oak, Auckland, New Zealand.

Sovereign Books, 14 Balmoral Road, Singapore 1025.

Struik Christian Books, PO Box 238, Salt River, 7925, South Africa.

Spring Arbor Distributors, 10885 Textile Road, Belleville, MI 48111, USA.

Canadian Christian Distributors, PO Box 550, Virgil, Ontario LO5 110, Canada.